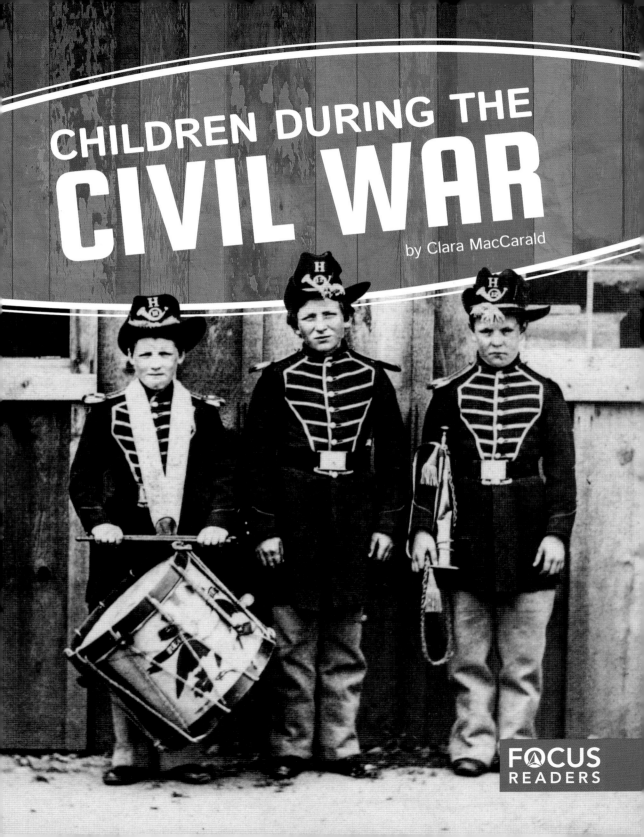

CHILDREN DURING THE
CIVIL WAR

by Clara MacCarald

FOCUS READERS

www.focusreaders.com

Focus Readers is distributed by North Star Editions:
sales@northstareditions.com | 888-417-0195

Produced for Focus Readers by Red Line Editorial.

Content Consultant: Robert I. Girardi, historian, lecturer, and author of nine books relating to the US Civil War.

Photographs ©: E. & H.T. Anthony/Library of Congress, cover, 1; North Wind Picture Archives, 4–5, 8–9, 13, 15, 21, 30–31, 42–43; Red Line Editorial, 7; Library of Congress, 11, 16–17, 41; Nancy Carter/North Wind Picture Archives, 19; Historic American Buildings Survey/Library of Congress, 23; Fisk University/John Hope and Aurelia E. Franklin Library/Special Collections, 24–25; James Wallace Black/Library of Congress, 29; Arthur Rothstein/FSA/Office of War Information/Library of Congress, 33; Chicago History Museum/Getty Images, 35; Major Moulthrop/Liljenquist Family collection/Library of Congress, 36–37; George Armistead/AP Images, 39; Wenderoth, Taylor & Brown/Liljenquist Family collection/Library of Congress, 44

ISBN
978-1-63517-872-2 (hardcover)
978-1-63517-973-6 (paperback)
978-1-64185-176-3 (ebook pdf)
978-1-64185-075-9 (hosted ebook)

Library of Congress Control Number: 2018931672

Printed in the United States of America
Mankato, MN
May, 2018

ABOUT THE AUTHOR

Clara MacCarald is a freelance writer with a master's degree in biology. She lives with her family in an off-grid house nestled in the forests of central New York. When not parenting her daughter, she spends her time writing nonfiction books for kids.

TABLE OF CONTENTS

CHAPTER 1

WAR BETWEEN THE STATES

In the mid-1800s, the United States was a nation divided by slavery. In the slave states of the South, slavery was legal. But in the North, most states did not allow it. However, racism existed in both the North and South. Many white people believed black people were an inferior race.

In November 1860, Abraham Lincoln was elected president. His political party was against the idea of allowing slavery in new US territories.

Citizens in Charleston, South Carolina, watch the attack that began the Civil War.

People in the South worried that Lincoln would also take away states' rights to keep slavery legal.

After Lincoln won the election, 11 of the 15 slave states **seceded** from the United States. Together they formed the Confederate States of America. The states that remained part of the United States were known as the Union.

In April 1861, Confederate soldiers attacked a government fort. The attack marked the beginning of the US Civil War (1861–1865). Lincoln told the public that the war was about keeping the United States together, not about slavery.

Of the three million soldiers that fought in the conflict, as many as 420,000 were children. Boys under the age of 18 could **enlist** with their parents' permission. Many others lied about their age. After **emancipation** in 1863, approximately 180,000 black soldiers also fought for the Union.

At home, children feared for their relatives on the battlefields. Many children worked to help support their families. The destruction of war created many **refugees**. Food and other goods became scarce, and diseases spread. No child went through the war untouched.

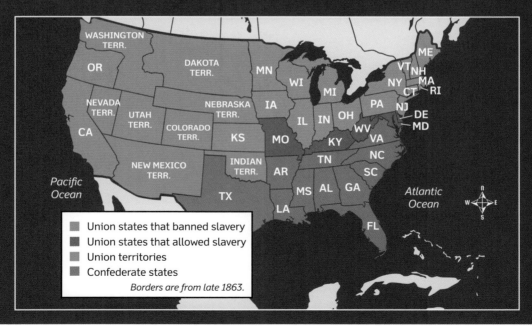

THE UNITED STATES DURING THE CIVIL WAR

Union states that banned slavery
Union states that allowed slavery
Union territories
Confederate states

Borders are from late 1863.

CHAPTER 2

UNDER SIEGE

Born in 1852, Lida Lord lived with her family in Vicksburg, Mississippi. Her family owned two enslaved women, as well as the children of one of the women. When the Civil War broke out, Lida's father did not enlist in the Confederate army. As a **rector**, he stayed home to run his church and take care of the people in Vicksburg. But even though Lida's father did not go to war, the war came to Lida's family.

Union soldiers built huts to sleep in during the attack on Vicksburg, Mississippi.

Mississippi was a member of the Confederacy, and Vicksburg was a key town controlling the Mississippi River. As the Union army approached in 1863, Confederate soldiers and their vehicles packed into the town. Some soldiers even slept on Lida's front porch, waiting for the battle to begin.

Union ships started bombing Vicksburg from the Mississippi River on May 22, 1863. Lida could hear the bombs explode. One night, the family was preparing dinner when an explosion shook the house. A bomb had landed on the dining room table, where everyone would have been sitting if the bomb had landed a few minutes later. Lida and her family fled the house.

To escape the bombs, people in Vicksburg dug caves in the hills surrounding the town. Lida's family squeezed into a series of short, connected tunnels with several other families. Boards and

▲ After the Siege of Vicksburg, the Union army built fortifications in the city.

screens separated the tunnels into sleeping areas. Lida slept on a bed of boards. From the cave, families watched the flash of bombs all night and heard their explosions all day.

One bomb collapsed a cave entrance. In terror, the people inside almost **stampeded**. Lida's family decided to move. They set up tents at the edge of town, near the safety of the city hospital.

Many nights, the family slept in their tents. But when bombs soared overhead, the family took shelter in a cave that had been dug by Confederate officers.

As a rector, Lida's father led services in his church every day, even when the bombs fell. Lida and her family also spent time with the soldiers. But beyond these activities, there was little for Lida to do. She was often either bored or terrified. One time, a shell nearly hit her younger brother. Another time, she found a rattlesnake underneath her mattress.

Hunger and exhaustion took their toll on the Confederate soldiers protecting Vicksburg. On July 4, 1863, they surrendered to the Union. Lida and her family returned to town to see the Union army marching through the streets. Many of the city's buildings were destroyed.

The fall of Vicksburg reopened the Mississippi River to Union ships.

Rather than stay in the defeated city, Lida and her family boarded boats alongside wounded Confederate soldiers. The family headed to New Orleans, Louisiana, which was under Union control. From there, the Lords moved to other cities in the South. At one point, Lida's father joined the Confederate army as a **chaplain**. After the war, the family finally returned to Vicksburg to help rebuild the city.

OPIE READ

Opie Read lived in Gallatin, Tennessee, during the Civil War. In 1862, when Opie was nine years old, Union forces approached his Confederate town. Opie begged a Confederate soldier on horseback to bring him along. "We rode forth to battle," he later wrote. "The morning was beautiful."

Opie and the soldier reached their destination just in time. The battle was about to begin. "Over the brow of a green slope, the enemy was advancing," he wrote. "I glanced to my right and saw that our men were stretched out on a long line, and looking ahead discovered that the enemy was in a similar form." The soldier with Opie blew his bugle as the battle started. Opie wrote that the two lines of soldiers met with a clash.

The triumphant Confederate troops chased off the Union soldiers. However, a stray shot killed the soldier that Opie had met. Opie fled for home.

⬥ Union and Confederate cavalry duel in a Civil War battle.

"I got in the saddle and rode up to a fence, got down, and ran back over the grassy slope," he wrote. The boy's beloved cousin was also among the Confederate dead left on the battlefield. Victory had come at a terrible cost.

Opie Read. *I Remember*. New York: Richard R. Smith, 1930. Print. 11–12.

CHAPTER 3

THE FREEDOM TO TEACH

Susie Baker was born in Georgia in 1848 to enslaved parents. When Susie was eight years old, the slaveholder who owned her family allowed Susie to move to Savannah, Georgia. She moved in with her grandmother, a free black woman. However, laws required free black people to have a legal guardian. Laws also limited when black people could travel. In addition, it was illegal to teach black people how to read and write.

Susie Baker went on to become a nurse, educator, author, and activist.

Despite the law, free black women in Savannah ran secret schools to teach black children. If the police discovered the schools, they might have shut them down. Susie pretended to be on errands so she could sneak into her teacher's house.

Susie learned as much as she could from the secret schools. Later, two white children broke the law to teach her. Susie used her knowledge to write fake travel passes. These papers allowed her grandmother to travel at night.

After the war started, 13-year-old Susie was sent back to live with her mother. Susie was curious to see Union soldiers. She had overheard

> **THINK ABOUT IT**

How would your life be different if you lacked the ability to read and write?

▲ Before the American Revolution, St. Simons Island was home to a British military fort.

her parents saying that the Union would end slavery. Susie soon got her wish. Susie escaped with her uncle's family to St. Simons, an island off the coast of Georgia. The Union had captured the island from the Confederate army. Union soldiers made a camp there for people freed from slavery.

One day, a Union officer discovered that Susie could read. He arranged for her to start a school at the camp. Susie taught dozens of children on the island. And in the evenings, she taught adults.

These individuals had not been allowed to attend school growing up. They were eager to learn how to read.

In June 1862, Confederate troops invaded the island, trying to take it back. Any black people they captured would be enslaved, even if the people had been free before escaping to the island. Black men from the camp fought off the Confederate soldiers while waiting for Union soldiers to arrive.

In September 1862, President Lincoln declared that all enslaved people in the Confederate states would be freed on January 1, 1863. The order was known as the Emancipation Proclamation. The Union also began allowing black men to enlist in the army. Because of the bravery of the men on St. Simons Island, the Union raised a black **regiment** there.

△ Freed black people march with Union soldiers after the Emancipation Proclamation.

When Susie was 14, she married a black sergeant. She also became a nurse, following the army with her husband and brother. After the South lost the war, Susie returned to Savannah. There, she started a school for black children. She gave them the opportunity to learn, which was a right that black people had previously been denied.

SUSIE BAKER

After the war, Susie Baker wrote a book about her life. In it, she recalled what it was like to live during the Civil War. Susie's white neighbors in Savannah had told her that the Union treated enslaved people terribly. But her grandmother told Susie they were lying. "The white people did not want slaves to go over to the Yankees," Susie remembered her grandmother saying. *Yankees* was a name for people who lived in the North.

Still, the black people in Savannah hung their hopes on the Union. "Oh, how those people prayed for freedom!" Susie wrote. One night, her grandmother attended a church meeting with other black people. "The police came in and arrested all who were there, saying they were planning freedom," Susie wrote. Her grandmother had to be released from jail by her guardian.

Union soldiers of the 48th New York Infantry line up at Fort Pulaski in 1863.

Union soldiers attacked nearby Fort Pulaski on April 1, 1862. "I was sent out into the country to my mother," Susie wrote. "I remember what a roar and din the guns made. They jarred the earth for miles. The fort was at last taken by them."

After the attack, Susie fled to the safety of St. Simons. She would never again have to live under slavery.

Susie King Taylor. *Reminiscences of My Life in Camp with the 33d United States Colored Troops Late 1st S. C. Volunteers.* Boston: Susie King Taylor, 1902. Print. 8–9.

CHAPTER 4

FREEDOM BUT NOT EQUALITY

Ella Sheppard was born into slavery in 1851 in Tennessee. Both of her parents were also enslaved. However, Ella's father was determined to free the family. To make that happen, he needed money. He planned to buy the family's freedom.

Many white people did not hold slaves. But these people sometimes paid slaveholders to use their slaves for part-time jobs. Slaveholders usually kept most of the money from this work.

Ella Sheppard (left) sits with her younger sister.

However, some allowed the enslaved person to keep a small amount. Ella's father slowly earned money in this way. Over time, he saved enough to buy his own freedom. He continued saving money, hoping to buy freedom for Ella's mother next.

When Ella was three years old, her father's plan failed. The slaveholders said they would never

➤ SLAVERY IN THE UNITED STATES

1619
English colonists first bring enslaved black people to Virginia.

1775
The first US group opposing slavery is formed. It is called the Society for the Relief of Free Negroes Unlawfully Held in Bondage.

1777
Vermont becomes the first state to ban slavery in its state constitution.

1787
The US Constitution is signed, putting into place protections for slavery.

1863
The Emancipation Proclamation frees enslaved people in the Confederate states.

1865
The Thirteenth Amendment bans slavery in the United States.

sell Ella's mother. But Ella's mother convinced the slaveholders to sell Ella to her father. Two years later, Ella's father paid for the freedom of a different woman. He then married her.

As Ella grew older, her father believed it was important for her to start school. Tennessee did not have laws against teaching black people to read and write. However, white people often threatened black schools. Ella and other students had to sneak to class to keep its location secret. Despite their efforts, city leaders eventually closed all schools for black children.

Legally, Ella's father owned his daughter and wife. But he owed people money, and he feared they might try to take his family away as a form of payment. To keep everyone safe, Ella's father moved the family to Cincinnati, Ohio, where slavery was illegal.

Ella no longer had to fear being enslaved. Even so, the family did not find equality. Many black people lived in an unhealthy part of Cincinnati that had polluted water. Ella was often sick. When she was feeling well, she attended a public school for black students. However, she still had to have music lessons in secret.

When Ella was 10 years old, the Civil War started. Ohio stayed in the Union, but many white people in the state opposed the war. Many of them also supported slavery. During a **strike** in the city, white workers became angry with black workers for taking low-paying jobs. White mobs roamed areas of town where black people lived. They broke windows and started fires.

Some black people fought back, and people on both sides were armed. Children such as Ella had to hide or escape the violence. After a week,

▲ Ella (fourth from right) and the Jubilee Singers sang hymns that many black people had sung while enslaved.

authorities managed to restore calm to the city. But Ella had learned she couldn't trust the white people of Cincinnati.

After the war, Ella returned to Tennessee to visit her mother, who was now a free woman. Later, Ella attended college. She then became a member of a famous singing group, the Jubilee Singers, and traveled throughout the United States and Europe.

CHAPTER 5

ANGER IN THE NORTH

Edwin Fitzgerald was born in 1856 in New York City. Like many residents of the city, Edwin's parents had moved to the United States from Ireland. Many parts of New York City could be dangerous. Gangs sometimes fought in the street. Poor people often lived in crowded, unsafe buildings. However, Edwin's family was fortunate. They lived in pleasant rooms above his father's tailor shop.

An angry crowd burns down an orphanage for black children in the 1863 New York draft riots.

When Southern states started seceding in late 1860 and early 1861, New York City considered leaving the Union as well. Businesses in the city relied on the South as a source of customers and raw materials. White workers also feared that free black people would move north to take their jobs.

However, by the time fighting began, members of President Lincoln's political party had gained support in New York City. That meant the city's government now supported the Union. Edwin and his parents watched soldiers parade down the streets. With bands playing and flags waving, the war seemed exciting.

Edwin's father decided to enlist. But after a few months, he was removed from the army because of health problems. Unfortunately, he died soon after returning to the city. With Edwin's father gone, the family had very little income. They

▲ Young boys continued to take on jobs as bootblacks well into the 1900s.

moved to a smaller home, and the children took jobs. Edwin became a **bootblack**. He wandered the streets offering to polish men's boots. He often danced to attract customers.

By 1863, thousands of people had been wounded or killed in the war. The Union needed more soldiers, so the government started a **draft** for men between the ages of 20 and 45. However, white people in New York City hated the draft.

They thought it was unfair, especially because rich men could pay $300 to avoid military service. Black men weren't included in the draft at all.

On July 13, 1863, mobs started a riot in the streets. The mobs aimed some of their violence at city officials and rich people. However, most of their violence was directed toward black people and their supporters. All over town, there were reports of fires, destruction, and deaths.

Edwin slipped out of his house to witness the riots. He watched people fight with clubs and bricks, but then gunshots scared him into hiding. On his way home, he saw a dead body.

➢ THINK ABOUT IT

Why did rioters turn their anger about the draft toward black people?

▲ Edwin Fitzgerald, later known as Eddie Foy, went on to act in comedy shows across the United States.

After four days of riots, city police and Union soldiers calmed the city. Scared by what had happened, Edwin's mother moved the family hundreds of miles away to Chicago, Illinois.

Years after the war ended, Edwin took his footwork from the streets to the stage. He became a famous performer who went by the name of Eddie Foy. But he never forgot the violence he experienced during the war.

CHAPTER 6

SOLDIER BOY

Ransom Powell was born in 1849 and grew up in Maryland. Although Maryland was a slave state, it stayed in the Union during the Civil War. At age 13, Ransom joined the Union army as a drummer boy. At first, drummer boys could join the war at any age. Later in the war, only older boys could join.

Ransom learned how to play different types of drum calls. Some called the soldiers to gather.

Drummer boys dressed in uniform and stood beside other soldiers on the battlefield.

Other calls signaled a retreat. A steady beat provided a rhythm for marching soldiers.

Aside from drumming, Ransom carried out chores. He fetched water and even helped the unit's doctor treat soldiers. By the age of 14, he had his own gun to carry.

Ransom's unit was stationed in West Virginia, a newly created state. West Virginia had been formed when supporters of the Union seceded from the Confederate state of Virginia. Ransom saw some fighting, but in January 1864, West Virginia was quiet. When Ransom learned about a wagon that needed a soldier escort, he immediately volunteered.

Ransom spent the quiet ride pretending he was shooting at Confederate soldiers. The 14-year-old bragged about how brave he would be in battle. But when Confederate soldiers burst into view,

▲ Drummer boys in the Union army gather at their camp after battle.

Ransom tried to run. The soldiers caught up and surrounded him, taking him prisoner. Soon, he and others from his unit were sent to a prison on Belle Isle in Virginia.

The facility was overcrowded with prisoners of war. The Confederate guards gave them only soup and cornbread to eat. The starving Union soldiers nearly froze in the tents they were forced to live in.

As a young person, Ransom was treated a little better. He had more food than the other soldiers. Occasionally, the Confederates would take him and other children on trips outside the prison.

In the spring, Ransom was sent to a train station with other Union soldiers. Some men lacked shoes and warm clothing to wear in the chilly weather. Eventually, the soldiers arrived in Georgia at the gates of Camp Sumter, also known as Andersonville prison.

Andersonville prison was built by enslaved people on a remote spot in the countryside. More than 30,000 Union soldiers were kept in a space designed to hold only 10,000. Inside the prison, cruelty, disease, and hunger were common.

Ransom was luckier than many of the soldiers. For several months, he lived with Confederate soldiers instead of staying in the prison. Ransom

A Prisoners at the Andersonville prison lived in small, makeshift huts.

ate well and went for outings. He often visited the prison to see his old comrades and try to keep up their spirits. Eventually, Ransom was sent back to live in the prison. But by then, most of his friends had died from the terrible conditions.

Later that year, Ransom was sent home. He was so sick he ended up at a hospital. After the war had ended, he formally left the military at the age of 16. Years later, he wrote about his experiences as a soldier and a prisoner.

CHAPTER 7

A NATION REUNITED

Near the end of the war, the US Congress passed the Thirteenth Amendment to the Constitution. This amendment banned slavery across the United States. Approximately four million enslaved people would soon be free. On April 9, 1865, Confederate general Robert E. Lee surrendered to Union general Ulysses S. Grant. The Union army moved in to occupy the defeated states of the South.

Many freed black adults and their children sought education after the end of the Civil War.

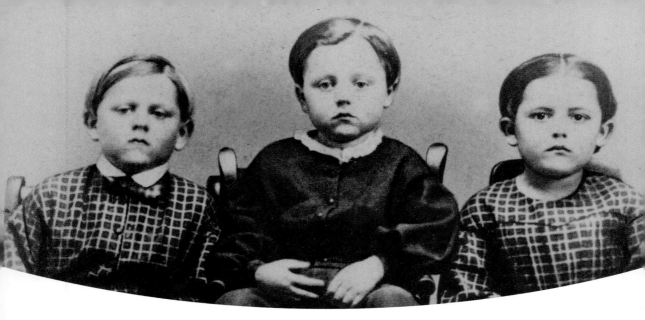

▲ The father of these children died on the battlefield holding this picture in his hands.

The fighting was over, but the effects of the war were not. Battles had destroyed homes and farms, bringing devastation to many Southern states. Cities lay in ruin. With approximately 620,000 soldiers dead, thousands of children had lost fathers and brothers.

Before the war, black families across the country had been torn apart by slavery. Now that slavery had ended, families looked for their lost relatives. In addition, many black families moved away from the South, hoping to find more equality in the North.

Various businesses helped rebuild parts of the South. In the North, the government worked to create jobs for struggling families. However, most families across the country were still very poor.

Though slavery had ended, many white people pushed back hard against black people's rights. White supremacist groups, such as the Ku Klux Klan, began to form. Black people, including children, faced anger and violence. The Civil War was over, but the black children who lived through it had to fight for equality for years to come.

THINK ABOUT IT ◁

Why didn't the end of slavery also end racism against black people?

FOCUS ON
CHILDREN DURING THE CIVIL WAR

Write your answers on a separate piece of paper.

1. Write a sentence that describes the key ideas of Chapter 1.

2. Do you think the Civil War was fought over slavery or to keep the United States together? Why?

3. Who surrendered to Union general Ulysses S. Grant?
> **A.** Edwin Fitzgerald
> **B.** Abraham Lincoln
> **C.** Robert E. Lee

4. Which statement is most accurate about the North's attitude toward slavery during the Civil War?
> **A.** Everyone in the North thought slavery was wrong.
> **B.** Some people in the North supported slavery, and others opposed it.
> **C.** More people held slaves in the North than in the South.

Answer key on page 48.

GLOSSARY

bootblack
A person who shines boots and shoes for money.

chaplain
A person who performs religious work for a hospital, school, prison, or military.

draft
A system for selecting people for required military service.

emancipation
The freeing of people from slavery.

enlist
Join the military.

rector
The leader of a church.

refugees
People forced to leave their homes due to war or other dangers.

regiment
A military unit.

seceded
Withdrew from a political union.

stampeded
Ran away in a panicked, uncontrolled way.

strike
When people stop working as a way to demand better working conditions or better pay.

TO LEARN MORE

BOOKS

Bailey, Diane. *The Emancipation Proclamation and the End of Slavery in America*. New York: Rosen Publishing Group, 2015.

Otfinoski, Steven. *The Civil War*. New York: Scholastic, 2017.

Shepard, Ray Anthony. *Now or Never!: Fifty-Fourth Massachusetts Infantry's War to End Slavery*. Honesdale, PA: Calkins Creek, 2017.

NOTE TO EDUCATORS

Visit **www.focusreaders.com** to find lesson plans, activities, links, and other resources related to this title.

INDEX

Answer Key: 1. Answers will vary; **2.** Answers will vary; **3.** C; **4.** B